WHAT IS, IS?
I WAS JUST THINKING.

MARTIN WILLIAM ANDERSON

Gotham Books
30 N Gould St.
Ste. 20820, Sheridan, WY 82801
https://gothambooksinc.com/
Phone: 1 (307) 464-7800

© 2022 Martin William Anderson. All rights reserved. No part of this book may be reproduced, stored in a retrieval system, or transmitted by any means without the written permission of the author.

Published by Gotham Books (September 24, 2022)

ISBN: 979-8-88775-076-7 P
ISBN: 979-8-88775-077-4 E

Any people depicted in stock imagery provided by iStock are models, and such images are being used for illustrative purposes only.

Certain stock imagery © iStock.

Because of the dynamic nature of the Internet, any web addresses, or links contained in this book may have changed since publication and may no longer be valid. The views expressed in this work are solely those of the author and do not necessarily reflect the views of the publisher, and the publisher
hereby disclaims any responsibility for them.

98.6.

Who's got that 98.6? I Need 98.6 like a dope fiend needs its fix.

You seem to think I need an intervention.

Did I forget to mention, I need 98.6 to relieve my anxiety and tension?

See, it runs deep through me like the roots of a tree run into the earth.

See, there is nothing better in this world when 98.6 is lying next to me.

When we're in the mix especially, 98.6 is the remedy.

It could be the cure for what is ailing me.

98.6 never failing me. See 98.6's heart is pure.

Just the right degree that makes my heart endure.

I love when 98.6 is next to me.

You'll be glad to know, that 98.6 is more;

you see, than just ecstasy.

A Disappointment

A disappointment I was said to be.
Not exactly what I thought of me.
Disappointing felt by him, she, and thee.
Members of my family tree.

You see that was not part of my plan.
Especially because I was on track to being "The Man".
Accomplishments I had more than a few.
A good career, 4-bedroom, 2 baths, with a pool home and a family.

With that success followed addictions, legal restrictions
and let's not forget adultery.
Lost all material things and my family.
The women and drugs were my Achilles heel.

Drugs and woman well, if you've had the unpleasant experience,
you know the deal.
Rehabbing my torn Achilles today.
Wreckage of my past still label me a disappointment some would say.
The road to recovery is not an easy one, you see.
But a disappointment, I am determined to no longer be.

A NEW NORMAL

Some may say unusual. Maybe considered just a little bit different.
Not just the same old song, often thought to be just plain ole wrong.
There are those who expect from you the same old thing.
Unsure of what exactly you may bring.

You see, they didn't anticipate a brand new you.
We're not at all aware of the things you can do.
This sudden surprise, not at all new to you.
Often believed not to be normal, yes this is true.

While you were hoping they would be accepting
of something new from you.
At the same time not being able to deal with a new you.

Normal, what is it really?
It seems something people hoped you would be.
Normal, what is normal? Seriously.
I'd love for you to explain it to me, personally.
Your definition is one that is different to me.

Normal apparently, I chose not to be.
Prefer young, wild, happy, with transparency.
All said and done I'm just fine with me.
So, screw your definition of normal whatever that may be.
By definition, your normal is too formal for me.
Simply put the truth is, I am a new normal. Can't you see?

AIN'T GONNA HAPPEN

Once upon a time I was Captain of the ship.
My first mate was there, we were joined at the hip.
One fog filled day a mutiny took place.
Not even a secret, right in front of my face.

Shiver me timbers they had me walk the plank.
Shackled in irons to the bottom I sank.
Wondering how I wound up in a virtual shark tank.
Asking the question, who thought up of this punishment?
What gave you the notion?

To render me helpless at the bottom of the ocean.
This wasn't how it was supposed to be.
We were trying to be a family,
destination the seven seas.

Apparently, the crew had other plans
and they didn't include me.
Now who will guide the ship?
Who is the new Captain?

One thing I know for me:
it ain't gonna happen.

ALL WE GOT IS ALL WE NEED!

We're all we got, we're all we need.
A mantra we should adhere to, If we believe.
With unity true success is guaranteed.
See, I need you and you need me.

We're all we got but we're all we need.
It's you and I against the world indeed.
To work together we must concede.

I'll try once again to plant this seed.
Some will contend they live by a better creed.
But I'm all you've got and you're all I need.

ASSHOLENESS

What's up?
Got yourself running around here
thinking and believing you're hot shit.
Don't even realize that you're full of it.

Now wait just one minute, I'll address that in a bit.
Coming around here trying to give everybody the biz.
Always talking big stuff, well let me tell you how it really is.

Think you can just come around here
trying to instill some type of fear.
Well sit back, chillax
and let me explain something to you my dear.

Just in case you didn't notice,
you ain't punking nobody here.
Running your mouth with what you think
is some sort of boldness.
Baby, what you really got is a bad case
of straight assholeness.

BABIES CHANGE EVERYTHING

From the moment you gazed into each other's eyes. Should have thought long and hard before you slid between those thighs. Congrats. Guess what? You have conceived.

For some this scenario can be hard to believe. See, the statement I'm about to make without a doubt is a sure thing. A baby, my friends, changes everything. First challenge is you never know what exactly this co-mingling will bring. A girl or a boy? Do I get pink or blue? Now you're sitting scratching your head asking yourselves what the hell did we just do?

Wow, do I have to train a woman or raise up a man? Wondering the whole time why you didn't have a plan. Babies change everything, you need to open your eyes. Went at it unprotected and now want to act surprised.

Babies coming down with something got you blaming each other. Grandmas asking why is the baby sick? Mama blaming the Daddy and Daddy blaming the Mother. Never saw this one coming.

Now baby's causing you to fight. Point fingers at each other; No, you stay home and watch him. It's my turn to go out to night.

Joy, love and pain, a baby's sure to bring. no longer singing lullabies, now it's the Blues you sing. You wouldn't listen to me then.

Now these words true to you should ring.

Like I tried to tell yo ass once before.

A baby changes everything.

BE REAL

When all else fails and all you have left is you.
Realize you need to consistently be yourself.
On that you need to rely and nothing or no one else.
Don't worry about how others view you.
Acceptance by outsiders no longer an issue.
Just be real and do you.

At the end of the day, you are the only one you need to answer to.
You can make it through anything if you're real with yourself.
How about trying for once to impress yourself.
This may fall under the category of self-help.

You came into this world all alone
and when you expire the real you will have been shown.
On display for all who knew you to critique.
Dissecting your past, knowledge of the real you they seek.

The first step that you need take to achieve the real you.
Is believe in yourself and to thine own self be true.
The one thing I've learned in my lifetime rings true.
The one hardest to deceive, is the real you.

I challenge you to lie to yourself
and you'll find it's something you can't do.
Now believe if you want that you can fool you.
Just give it a try you will see the real you.

You lying to you, it just can't be done.
Because you know the real.

BEST IN CLASS

I was told from the day of my birth.

How I lived my life would determine it's worth.

A lump of mere clay to be molded, you see.

Best in class from day one was expected of me.

Looking back at one time it seemed I was on the right track.

Veered off track could say I got derailed.

I didn't stay on the path, basically strayed from the trail.

The trail I chose led through the wrong pass.

My map led me to the wrong destination.

Asking myself why did you take that pass?

Took me to the worst place, a less than desirable destination,

a place commonly known as last.

No chance of being coveted with the title.

Best in class.

BETTER OR LESS?

In this lifetime you'll feel better sometimes maybe less.

One thing is clear, this life we live is certain to put you through tests.

As for the Law it is designed to hold you to the letter.

When it does, question is do you feel less, or do you feel better?

It is one of life's tests that is designed to protect you.

For some it seems this thing they call justice may often neglect you.

Do you feel better or less when it comes to your maturation?

If so, then why do you tend to feel less

about life's often times mis-education.

Tell me, does it lead to better or less of your personal concentration? These tests life gives, do you find yourself in better situations?

Or do you continually lead a life filled with better or less frustration.

To tell you the truth regarding your request.

I can honestly say I don't know if I feel better or less.

BIG MOUTH

I admit, I've got one; this is true. But after listening to you, I realize I'm not the only one; it seems you've got a big mouth too.
You said I was spilling the family business to strangers. This one time, only a sentence.
Turns out that sentence caused relationship danger.

Mama always told me never talk to strangers. I repeat it was only a sentence.
Unfortunately, our love verdict a death sentence, even with remorse shown and also repentance.

I tried to apologize for the words that were said.
Don't you understand I wanted to put this bull shit to bed?
But noooo, you just couldn't accept it.
Your only mission in life was to make me regret it.

Calling me over and over made me feel like Red Rover. Just another dog you said.
Didn't know one little sentence could screw with your already messed up head.

Funny you can't remember what your big mouth said.
Let me refresh your memory, please allow me to help you.

"Nigga you should've ate your gun, your sister was a whore".

Truth is, all of that is true. It amazes me how you can talk shit about me,
but how dare me talk about you. One difference is my sister the whore was smarter than the two daughters raised by you.
At least when she got laid, she had sense enough to get paid.
Whereas the two whores your daughters turned about to be, gave their valuables away for free.

For the last time, I've got a big mouth and I know this to be true.
What you need to do, is humble yourself and admit…
you've got a big mouth too.

Now listen very close because this is about to go twelve rounds.
Just be aware you're going against one of the best there is, pound for pound.
Instead of wasting my time continuing to fuss and fight with you.
Let me be the one to say first: Bitch I'm thru with you.

The reason is crystal clear to me:
You've got a big mouth
bigger than mine could ever be.

I'm done with you
and after this I know
your punk ass
is done with me.
BIG MOUTH!!!!!!!!!!!!!!!!!

BLAME IT ON ME

So here we are again, you want to talk about me.

Trying to make feel like a dunce.

Naw, not today, always blaming me for the problems in this relationship. For once we're going to flip the script.

Today is not about me. Let's talk about you.

I'll give you this, nine times out of ten

you make it do what it does when it comes to you.

As a matter of fact, you have a knack of turning something out of nothing. The pettiest of things that are nothing you twist and turn into something.

Lately I see you hanging with your frenemies', poor thing.

Sad thing is, I recall when you used to be a friend of me.

Now all of a sudden nothing to me.

Not even somewhat like they use to be.

For quite some time it was just you and me.

Later found out free of me you truly wanted to be.

The problem is and has always been, your ways and you.

Can't you see? Knowing you, you probably can't.

So, I'll quit and go back to your original script

and let you just blame it all on me.

BLANK PAGES

Just like my life attempting to fill in the blanks.
When it comes to God always forgetting to give thanks.
At times it's because things in life seem to push me toward rages.
Just appears never could live life in any sort of good stages.
See, in every stage of my life, at one time or another
war has been waged.

It wasn't always like this; some stages went well.
Then there were others, which put me through hell.
With the stages there appeared to me no type of stagger.
They ran so closely together it disrupted my swagger.
A stage without steps, never should there be.
With no steps to the stage, a fall is a certainty.

I'd find myself asking "how did this happen to me"?
You missed a crucial line of the play, don't you see?
You failed to follow instructions given by he.
"Who's he"? you ask, he's God don't you know?
He's the director, composer, and creator of your life's show.

You were told to memorize the script he wrote long ago.
"I've never read the script; it was never given to me".
Do you not recall? we rehearsed the lines every day.
From the script entitled the B.I.B.L.E. written to show you the way.

Follow the script he has written and be the star of life's show.
It was designed to take you places, most never will go.
So, stop improvising, stop being a flop.
His play's written for you.
Was created to put you on top.
So have faith in his word, created especially for you.
It's a well written plan that will take you through stages.
If you stick to the script, you will fill life's blank pages.

BLESSING?

A blessing, that's what I thought she was.
I first met her while at the club.
Her face and that swagger, all the buzz.

One glance her way was all it took.
A wink and a smile my way,
well let's just say
I was hooked.

You see, I saw her as a blessing.
My eyes began undressing.
Soon after we began messing.
Had no idea the number of years with her,
I'd be stressing.

A blessing, yeah right,
all we did was fuck, fuss and fight.
Still in my mind thinking
all would be alright.
But with her mind I couldn't tell
if it was day or night.

Praying for her to disappear from sight.
Misguided I was to believe her a blessing.
Never imagined the misery that blessing would bring.

I must admit, I'm truly confessing.
Next time I will pray for God's guidance.
Before I assume it's a blessing.

BREAK ME OUT

Please can someone please help break me out?
Where do I begin? Out of this makeshift prison my heart and mind are in.
They've been locked up so long I don't know where it all started or if it will end.
Once they both were considered two of my close's friends.
Problem is, they lead me down a road that turned out to be a dead end.

It was supposed to be a trip, one of peace and joy.
Accompanied by beautiful women, libation and party favors
designed for recreation.
While on this excursion I found out they both lied to me.
The women, immoral. Displaying anger and loving to quarrel.
Libations led to trouble and multiple incarcerations;
you may ask: But what about the sensations?

I don't quite remember, but I recall some suspect penetration.
Party favors I began to crave. Rendered powerless I became enslaved.
This addiction has me with one foot in the grave.
None of this was a part of the plan.

Once stood tall on a rock, now on sinking sand.
Turned out they both made a fool of me.
Blinded by their allure could no longer see. Mind twisted heart broken.
Any fond memories, a meaningless token.
Convicted and found guilty by my mind, heart and soul you see.

Verdict, imprisonment by all three, I was sentenced to be.
No doubt there was a woman behind the scenes manipulating me.
She started with my heart then played tricks with my mind.
Had me believing no greater love I'd find.
Seemed everything was good but somethings a miss.
"There's nothing wrong baby." She would often insist.

Now serving a life sentence with no chance parole, no doubt.
Down on my knees finally.
Begging God please, can you break me out?

CAN I BE A MEMBER?

What's it takes to be a member of your club?

I heard that membership has its privileges.

You're asking me if a member I would like to be?

I'll do better that. I want to be a V.I.P.

At your private club just you and me.

Oh, what a privilege that would be.

The best thing about having our members meet at your private club.

You better believe there'll be some rub a dub dub.

At the bar on the floor and definitely the hot tub.

So once again, how do I become a member of your V.I.P. club.

Don't even consider giving me the snub.

Now I know there are many clubs in different villages.

The difference is membership in your club has its privileges.

CAN WE TALK?

I was wondering can I talk to you?

Sitting here, trying to figure out what you and I could do, about me and you.

I'd really like to know. Girl when you and I connect.

Damn, the blood just starts to flow.

My mind begins to race.

Then slows down to snap a mental picture of your lovely face.

My heart well, let's just say it's trying to keep pace.

All the while asking where's my place?

My body stuck I can't even walk.

I just have one question miss lady.

Can we talk?

CAN'T DO ALL THINGS RIGHT IN LIFE!

You can't do all things right in life.
All you can do is live it.
You know that seems to ring true.
I can't seem to do anything right in in my life.
Is it just me or is it you too?

Seems in life you can give all you have, or a little bit.
It will turn out how he planned, still trying on your feet to land.
You can't control it.

Should just go ahead and live it.
When will you realize this journey, you're on
is filled with stress and strife.

No matter how hard you try you can't do all things right in life.

Carve Your Successes in Stone & Your Failures in The Sand.

Why is that?
You may ask.
It would seem to be such a difficult task.
Successes in life are hard to obtain.
If carving in sand, you should refrain.
Yet, carved in stone sure to remain.

Failures carved in sand the tides of life will wash away.
Successes in stone are here to stay, for all to see day after day.

Do not build your dreams on sinking sand.
Stick to those carved in stone,
hold them tightly in your hand.

Remember they were not carved in sand.
So, you and success will forever stand.

So, when you wonder how this can be?
Carved in stone you chose to be.

CHANGES

Going through changes my mind is,

trying to figure out what it's going through this time around.

See, it once was lost, then believed to be found.

It's seems the road I'm on, I've already been.

Road traveled once, please not again.

You see, I've been there, done that, have a Tee shirt and the DVD.

Road traveled once, maybe twice on second thought

I believe it's been three.

A road less traveled I wish it'd be.

I can't understand these constant changes.

Thinking once again what in the blazes.

Tried to think of them as my life in stages.

So many and so different they appear in hazes.

It may sound strange to you,

but I only wanted one last change in my life, you see.

The change I desire, is for a change in me.

COME CLEAN

Come clean, do you think you can do that?

I mean, tell me the truth without omitting the facts.

I mean, that's what you request of me.

Well, I expect the same from you.

I heard tell somewhere, to thine own self be true.

Constantly asking me to come clean,

no problem I'm an open book.

I verify my story, no need for a second or closer look.

I always come clean;

can I say the same for you?

Do you think, for once in your life, that is something you could do?

I mean, I mean:

Can you just come clean?

DAMN

You know, I've been asking quite some time for a simple picture of you. Just one, maybe two to etch in my mind. A picture of Luree.

A daily ritual, it is searching through my cell's gallery. Hoping, praying, and wishing today is the day just one pic of you I see.
Every day consistently yes this is true. Asked just as often what it is that I'm looking for? Answer to that question? A simple one: You!

Heard a beep from my phone one day wondered who could this be? Picked up, took a glance, ah shit, it's from Luree.

Thinking just some uplifting words, a bible quote, or two.

Opened it up well I'll be damn! Finally, my prayer's come true.

A rare birthday pic of you, clothes I guess were optional.

Sent a shock from my optical to my thing which started tingling.

When I say: Thing, I mean my ding a ling.

Checked again, not one, not two, but three.

Jaw-dropping shots of you there would be.

Now I'm horny, phone on fire, fingers scrolling hella fast.
But before I go just let me say on that last pic.
Damn, that's one nice ASS!!!!

DEAL WITH THIS

First thought was that this can't miss.

However, after some scrutiny and close analysis.

I was forced to question; do you really want to deal with this?

Thought it was love.

As you well know, that can be hit or miss.

Did everything in my power to reach the city of your Atlantis.

Now don't you be fooled; this is the truth that I speak.

I gave it the old college try at a life filled with bliss.

Asking the question, do you really want to deal with this?

Kids on her team and I'm not the baby daddy.

Influence everything that we did even just trying to be happy.

Sad at the fact opportunities missed.

Keeping it real, hell naw, can't deal with this.

DESPAIR

Despair, can you feel it in the air?
It's here, it's there, it's everywhere.
Make you think your life's a dare.

Despair will try to draw you in,
let it get close enough, you'll think it's a friend.
Despair itself just doesn't care.

Have you believing life's just not fair.
Leaving you just trying to cope when deep inside you have no hope.
So, when you're feeling totally fed up.
Use the phrase keep your head up.

Truth is that life is just not fair.
Despair will continue to try to make you give up hope.
Just when you've finally learned to cope.

Don't let despair dictate how you live.
In defeating it you must give all you have to give.

So, if you find yourself in the mirror with that faraway stare.
The one that says you no longer care.

Come back my friend.
Don't go there, your bordering on the place called despair.

DO YOU BELIEVE?

Do you believe? you must.

All the things that you've been through.

Do you still dream of catching that Great White Whale?

To live long enough to tell the tale.

Do you believe when caught, you can survive on its blubber?

Long enough until you can land another.

You say that you believe things are going to get better.

You don't know why, but you still believe.

Even while navigating through stormy weather.

Why is it, that you believe that you are bound to drown?

Believing you were lost and now you're found.

What can you do to once again believe in you?

This one fact you will find to be true.

Simply put, believe in He who always believes in you.

That's the only thing you need to do.

Do you believe?

DON'T GO THERE

I guess the first question is: Why can't I?

No, seriously. Seems like you don't even want me to try.

You can't go there, at times that's true.

But who are you to tell me what I can or cannot do?

See, I feel like life presents some tests.

It will push to a point where you have to prove that you are the best.

It will remind you that you can't go there.

I already know it doesn't seem fair.

Ask life's opinion you'll find it really doesn't care.

My challenge to you if you dare.

Buckle up, strap in tight, and be the one who dares to go there.

EPISODES

Episodes, I must admit, I have them sometimes;

What about you?

Come on, admit it, you have episodes too.

See, an episode can have you trying to figure out

who to blame.

Family, friend's... hell, even a made-up name.

Episodes, even the next aren't all the same.

Have an episode bad enough, may forget your own name.

To be continued tomorrow, so stay tuned.

For the next episode caption reads,

coming soon.

EXPERIENCE

It's been said, experience, is the best teacher.
I believe they are right.
I am no dummy, I was born at night
but it wasn't last night.

See, experience has been not just a Teacher
but more of a Professor to me.
In fact, experience has helped me earn my B.S.,
My Masters and I'm currently working on my thesis for my P.H.D.

Experience is a discipline in higher learning.
Fail an exam or a final, for a retake you'll be yearning.
Experience has taught me a lot.
It opened my eyes to such things as loss.

The loss of my only sibling.
Loss of friends and family.
A 30-year marriage, great career, homes,
cars, relationships, and reputation.

In total frustration, I improved my skills.
Minoring in bull shit, with a Major in lack of communication.

I had to ask experience: What's the deal?
You were supposed to teach me many things.
You forgot the lessons on the trials, tribulations and pain life brings.

In this life my experience is not all that I thought.
Professor asked: "Are you prepared for your next class?"
My answer: "No thanks, I've already been taught".

Oh yeah, about the next class.
I need to go to the bathroom.
"Can a brother please get a pass?"

EXTANT

Opposite of extinct.

Thoughts, words, and actions could eliminate me.

How did you think that would come to be?

Apparently, you have no idea of who I've come to be.

Extinct yes, you tried to make me.

It may have made sense in your mental,

but my game is too fundamental.

Extinct you will never make me.

Not in a lifetime, nor in your existence.

I am extant.

I will forever remain existent.

FAMILY TREE

Something very special to me.
Similar to an Old Oak or Redwood tree.
With roots that are both strong and deep.
Promises made, for souls to keep.

Its branches spread both far and wide.
This family is always by your side.
Storms will come, some branches and leaves may fall;
the loss of these affect us all.

Through the grace of GOD new leaves will sprout.
For he gives and he takes, without a doubt.
Just continue to pray and just think back.
How you stayed in prayer, when you felt
the family tree was under attack.

You see, tragedy can bend that old Oak like a Weeping Willow.
With morning may come a tear-soaked pillow.
Now branches can be broken on a day like this.
Yearning for strength from the leaf we'll miss.

This storm like many will eventually pass
and we will see the sunshine again at last.
Never forget the branches and leaves that are yours and mine.
They are forever apart of our tree until the end of time.
Reaching towards the heavens for all to see.

So be proud to be a branch or a leaf
on your family's tree.

FAR AWAY

Far away my goals and dreams seem to be.

The victories in life to few and far between.

The losses however seem to pile up, do you know what I mean?

Hoping for a win, any win will do.

But it seems that dream once again

not meant to be for me, what about you?

Well, what do you know, another loss.

Feels like my life is just one big coin toss.

Today hoping for a win yet expecting to fail.

Still have the hammer working to drive home the nail.

Trying to rebuild this house of broken goals and dreams.

This I can honestly say.

That honey dew won't get accomplished today.

Not even thinking about tomorrow, it's just too far away.

FEAR

Praying one day to my Lord up above.
The one who blesses with grace, mercy, and love.
I expressed the fear I was having that day.
He told me "Stop talking, listen and believe what I say"

He began to explain the true meaning of fear.
He said "It's just **F**alse **E**vidence **A**ppearing to be **R**eal"
He said "Just sit back and listen my son.
Have you forgotten for you all the things that I've done?"

I said, "No Father, I don't know, I'm just scared."
He whispered, "Don't worry my child with the Holy Spirit you're paired." He asked, "Tell me son, what's the root of your fear"?
I murmured with shame, "Dying alone", producing a tear.

His warmth so soothing my mood transformed,
from fear to confidence and happiness.
I'm sorry I digress.

"My child, realize that you're never alone.
Wherever you are you're always with three.
The Spirit, my Son Jesus and let's not forget me"

I rose to my feet, to shout dance and cheer.
My Heavenly Father's with me.
So, there is no need to fear.

FIGURE IT OUT

Why? I don't know. I'm still trying no doubt.

Asking myself what's this all about?

It appears to me I just can't see.

What the past was, what today is or what tomorrow will be.

I just can't figure it out.

Some days, like a little kid I just sit and pout.

Pondering what it will take to obtain some clout.

Man, I just can't figure it out.

A longtime friend asked what it is that I couldn't figure out.

I said if I knew that I wouldn't be confused, don't you see.

Do me a favor if you figure it out can you please tell me?

FINALLY, DID IT

I've been trying for a long time,

quoting as if this world was mine.

I would place at your feet all that I own;

you've been so good to me.

Thanks Luther and Cheryl.

You see, this is something I wished I could do and show you proof.

I meant every word; they came straight from the heart.

Deny all you like, but that was my wish from the start.

I have been talking for years about how I was going to do this.

By this I mean this writing thing.

The joy of accomplishment I just knew it would bring.

All In the title "I Was Just Thinking".

That by what appeared to be only a dream,

has now become reality.

With these few lines I hope you can admit it

while mouthing the words;

Damn, that boy finally did it.

FRACTIONED

Broken into different parts.
Somewhat like a mathematical equation.
Fractions and Decimals may prove
to be challenging and frustrating.

See, one thing I do know is
one ½ + one ½ equals one whole.
At least by my math teacher I was told.

Looking back, one whole of me,
I could never seem to be.
You have to understand
the life I chose to live,
made me less than half the man
I was supposed to be.

I was in theory a walking,
talking fraction.
Just a piece of me.

A broken soul, with no glimpse
of what I used to be.
If you look closely you will see,
I am fractioned.

Hoping and believing
my life one day will equate
to the whole of me.

GAME OF CHANCE

Every day we play the game.

The game called life, its true name.

At times we hesitate to play.

Occasionally jumping headfirst into the fray.

This game called life is a game of chance.

Do you stay put or try to advance?

Since the day we are born the dice are rolled

seven come eleven, in faith we hold.

While this game of chance waiting to see unfold.

Some will win and some will lose.

Continue to play, some will choose.

Odds stacked against you this is true.

Why not go all in and bet on you?

Life Is a game of chance.

GRANNY

I used to have two, that unlike many, I actually knew.
All of a sudden on separate occasions and days,
my Grannies would no longer be.

Emotions of pain and sadness took over me.
They had gone up yonder.
God had set them free.

I had to ask myself "Was the sadness I felt,
about them or more about me?"
Thinking about it, me it turned out to be.

The hole in my heart can never be filled.
For the love of a Granny requires a very special skill.
Grannies seem to always sense when somethings wrong.
Can cheer you up with just the right words or the perfect song.

Don't get it twisted, they will correct you when you do wrong.
Her tender kiss and warm hugs so strong, seems to last as the day is long.
No one could ever take Granny's place.
Oh, how I miss her smiling face.
Almost as much as her reassuring embrace.

How I wish my Granny were here,
but she's with God now so
I'll have no fear
knowing that Granny's spirit is always near.

I Love you Granny.

HIS GIFT WILL MAKE ROOM FOR YOU

Have you ever felt like there was no more room at the inn? No rooms anywhere when it comes to you. If you have, just remember this, and don't ever forget.

There was a special gift addressed to you.

"For me? can't be".

You must believe what I say is true. Patience and faith these you will need. For the gift sent from above was designed for you indeed.

It might not be what you want, but at this point in your life, is probably Just what you need. To help reach your goals, dreams and help you succeed.

So, when you when you think there is no place for you. Not knowing just what to say or do. You must trust that this gift, will uplift.

It was sent to, well, you know who.

For this gift, **God's** gift,

will make room for you.

HOPE

Keep hope alive. A phrase quoted by Jesse.
I believe he coined it for when times get messy.
You're sure that you can't, but you certainly can.
For hope gives you the strength when you're weak to take a stand.

Life will try to take all hope from you.
But keep hope alive you'll be amazed at what you can do.
Constantly asking how do you keep hope alive?
When every day's a struggle just trying to survive.

Answer is with God and his Angels always by your side.
They are sure to help you with your strive to thrive.
So, when life deals you once again that hand
that you in your mind, can no longer stand.
When it tries to discourage and connive.

Stay prayed up my brothers and sisters and keep hope alive.

HOW BAD DO YOU WANT IT

How bad do you want it? was the question asked of me.
The answer "I'm not sure, let me see".
To obtain what I want, just what are the requirements?
I need to mull it over at this moment I'm quite content.
I was told for starters you will need to figure your intent.

This quest needs your undivided attention.
Patience and focus are the key, did I forget to mention?
You will also need to be inspired to acquire
what it truly is that you desire.

Well, these days I really don't desire too much.
There is nothing material I crave for or long to touch.
Nothing to obtain just so I can flaunt.
Some out there flaunt just to taunt.

See, what I want is nothing tangible.
It involves more of my spiritual.
It's something felt I've yet to feel.
Some may say it's unconventional.

You see, at this time in life.
I seek a marriage without a wife.
Some joy, peace and definitely love.
The kind of love from up above.

The kind of love not found on earth.
The one true love that knows my worth.
I want it bad, and I want it now.
I want my Lord to embrace me.

For all the world to see the love of GOD all over me.
He gave his son to set me free and in return I'll give him me.
The question was how bad do I want it?
My answer is I want it bad.
For God's love's the greatest Love I've ever had

I AM

I am who you thought I was.
Then realized I wasn't.
It doesn't mean you were wrong.
Chances are you weren't.

It doesn't mean that I am who you think I am.
I maybe somebody totally different.
Just asking, but would that really make a difference?

When you probably don't really give a damn
about who I was or really am.
But for future reference if you choose to care.
I am Martin William Anderson
formally known as the man.

The real question should be, if I dare, is who in the hell are you?
Where do you come from and just what do you do?
See, I've taken my time to do research all about you.
I found out some things. I wonder if they're true.

The way that it seems your whole life's
nothing more than a sham.
You have so many aliases;
you can't tell who is who.

Again, my name is Martin William Anderson
and I know who I am.
I'll ask one more time: Who in the hell are you?
While you figure out who is who,
I'm gonna keep making it do what it do.

I DID IT

She said that I did it. I don't believe her. But to tell the truth man I don't know. What exactly did I do? I swear I don't remember it must be bad because she promised we were through.

Whatever it was that I was doing. I thought that I was running it. But a few foul words from her tells me I wasn't running shit.

She started finger pointing trying to force me to admit it. Kept on insisting I confess that I had did it. Still not knowing what the accusation contained so from admitting I abstained.

Pondering, wondering, racking my brain. The line of questioning driving me insane. Continuing to deny it all maintaining a defense. Feeling no need for recompense.

Still no idea of what I had done, she produces a photo of a mother and son. Looked very closely at the woman and kid. Oh damn, "eureka" now I know what I did.

I kept my defense still refused to admit it. But one look at that boy, had to say damn. Yeah, I did it.

I EARNED MY MISTAKES

Can't tell if there were few or many.
If my had my way, trust and believe there wouldn't be any.
How many licks does it take to get to the center of precision?

Exactly what does it take to sift through all the flakes and shaky Jakes?
So that next move I make is not a mistake.
To tell you the truth, I feel like I've been raked over the coals.

This young man's heart, mind and body feel old
not to mention my soul.
I made some mistakes and yes, I did earn them.
If it were up to me, I'd give all that I have to try and unlearn them.

See, mistakes are somewhat like rolling the dice.
Have you shaking your head wondering
if you should've thought it twice?

Like I told you before, hope you learn from your mistakes.
My mistakes one thing from them I learned.
There is not one mistake you make, that you will not earn.

I NEED A REASON?

You say that I need a reason to love someone.
Believed by me to be sent from above.
I need a reason?
Demanding that I explain myself.

First, it takes more to take care of someone than wealth.
Yes, I understand that is what you expect me to have.
Truth is, it is no longer the days of your dear old Dad.

Expected to provide for you and me.
Times have changed it takes two, even three
most times to support a family.

I realize for me financially things
have been both good and bad.
Fortunately, you've never experienced
the losses I've had.

You're lucky, like they say,
you can't miss what you never had.
You seem to think
you don't need a reason to love me.
I can tell you one thing, what I need from you
doesn't involve money.

For me, it's the intangibles you possess.
Your smile, your laugh, your warm caress;
Most of all your tenderness.

See, for me you don't need
a reason for loving me.
You wanting to be by my side
is reason enough for me.

I RAN

I can't remember when the track meet started. I just know I was young when I learned how to do it. It all began just trying to have fun. Didn't realize I was in training to run.

Running is all I wanted to do, anything I believed, it would get me through. Especially when I believed things wouldn't be fun. I'd put on my track shoes and begin to run.

Oh yes, and don't let things get tough I ran when I felt I'd had enough.

I ran from things I'd seen and done. I ran to not lose and pretend I'd won.

I had master plans that always failed. I ran to the bottle, the finish line jail. It seemed I was always running in my life.

I ran to the arms of another, from the loving arms of my wife. In the beginning I believed, it was just for some fun.

The trials and tribulations of that decision kept me on the run. Instead of believing in myself standing steadfast and taking advantage of an opportunity.

I ran from my friends, family and all responsibility. It was all just something to do when I began. Can't believe it took so long for me to finally understand.

GOD is the Way, Truth and the life. The time has finally come for once in my life to stop and take a stand. This is my last chance to change my life for good It's time to be a Man.

No longer can I wait. There is no debate. Trust in the LORD because what I can't do, he can. So, I put on the track shoes one last time and to the altar I ran.

I WAS JUST THINKING

I wanted to just try and write.
I needed to find a thought, maybe a word.
Asking myself, will this make sense or just seem absurd?
See, I was just thinking about the written and the spoken word.

Made me want to write about something
I may have seen or heard.
I was just thinking.

What if, there was something I wrote,
that could make things better for others.
The Fathers and Mothers, my sisters, and my brothers.
I was just thinking.

So, I took some time to write, while thinking,
my thoughts left some doubt,
of what it was I would write about.

So, I picked up a pen filled with ink,
only to remember, I was just thinking.
Just thinking.

I WRITE NOT RECITE

I don't recite, I write.
Let me explain, you might understand
why I'm better with a pen than a mic in my hand.

Now don't get me wrong, I understand the words that I write.
The problem is a bad memory makes it hard to recite.

I know what you think.
A brother got stage fright.
Not at all.

It's mastery of the written word
on the page in which you'll delight.
But without the written word in front of my face...
Let's just say my thoughts are all over the place.

The words that I write will seed you, feed you;
they'll make you realize
that you need to read them
over and over again.

Until they become like a long-lost friend.
When you read the words I write,
it allows you to be them.

Full of imagination, visualization, joy, wonder and insight.
You will see the beginning of something with no end.
It's not quite the same
when the words a recite.

I repeat once again
that I don't suffer from stage fright.
To those, to those doubting few.
I bid you adieu.
Hope you all have a good night.
I say for the last time.
I write, not recite.

I'M CLEVER?

Couldn't believe that is what she called me.

I gave it some thought and said" whatever".

You see, clever was just another word to me.

Clever I knew, I would always be.

I learned from clever how to be charming and to navigate.

However, clever failed to share the recipe to make me great.

There seems to be different levels that come with clever.

Never learned how to control the lever.

The one that takes you high and low

and gives you the insight you need to know.

When you need to stop or go.

Now looking back on some of the decisions in life that I have made.

My ego of clever appears to have been slayed.

Clever no longer do I claim to be,

I think I'll stick to being just plain ole me.

IMPROVEMENT!

They say practice makes perfect.
Well, I happen to disagree.
I say practice makes improvement
but hey, that's just me.

See, I can choose to improve or not.
Obtain what I want or settle for what I've got.
Choices between being a have or have not.

I just can't sit still.
I need to make some type of move.
One is necessary if I want to improve.

I must be decisive without hesitation.
With personal improvement I can raise
my level of concentration.

Just like Stella, I'm trying to get my groove back.
By working on improvement
there should be no problem achieving that.

There will be improvement
just you wait and see.
No practice just improvement,
no doubt I guarantee
is destined to bring out
the very best in me.

IN YOUR HANDS

It seems at times you really have it all.
At days end it's up to you whether you rise or fall.
You believe you have the whole world in your hands.
You want to make God laugh?
Well just make plans.

What's supposed to happen is to follow the path
he'd laid out for you.
If they tell you, you can make it on your own.
Let me be the first to say that's just not true.

See, once upon a time I thought I had the best laid plans.
It was then I realized it wasn't me but God who
has the whole world in his hands.

Yes, I know you might not quite understand.
So, I'll say it once again, he's got the whole world in his hands.
Mine, his, hers, and yes yours too.

Don't get me wrong.
Don't misunderstand.
He gives you free will to do what you want to.
So, when the day comes when
you believe it's time to take a stand.

Ventured from his laid-out path
and on your feet, you did not land.
Just remember the final outcome of that decision
was all part of your plan.

Unfortunately, you didn't leave your plan… in God's hands.

IRRITANT

Something that bothers you.
May be me, maybe you.
Come to think of it,
an irritant I just may be.

If I am honest with myself
this is definitely true.
An Irritant sometimes
resembles me.

However, for me it also resembles you.
Irritating not necessarily trying to be.
At times to tell the truth,
we both turn out to be.

I will tell you this,
if you keep bothering me you will see,
just how much of irritant
I can truly be.

So, on this one thing can we both agree.
I won't irritate you, if you don't irritate me.

IS IT ABOUT YOU?

Really don't care for all the fussing and fighting.
This is a subject that may need to be enlightened.
It always amazes me, write something
that a person knows is about them.
They know it's the truth,
want to say it's a lie
not knowing you have proof.

You try to explain
saying I didn't use your name.
It could be someone else
who did the exact same.

I didn't say it was you.
Standing there frowning,
your mood is blue.
All because what you read rings true.

You don't want to believe it,
yet you must receive it.
Upset because you know
it shows the true you.

You might as well get over it
because there will be more of it.
As long as you continue to do
the dirt that you do.

Not fussing or fighting
no longer with you.
No need to gloat,
I've already sunk your boat.

There ain't nothing you can do.
You must confess
you can't cleanup this mess.

The truth is boo.
It is about you.

IT TAKES A VILLAGE

It seems it took me a long time to see. Then one day I stopped, took a look, and couldn't believe what I saw. You had to be there to see for yourself, one child taking the time for someone else. A young man visiting a nearby neighbor, he went by the name of C.J.

I thought there just to play. By what I witnessed from C.J. let's just say he should be a fine man one day. See, the neighbors' young child was screaming and crying if I didn't know any better, could've sworn he was dying.

All because C.J. was going home the young child gave chase with a look of despair all over his face. C.J. stopped in his tracks, to turn and take a look, when he saw the young child his head he just shook. He picks the boy up; his goal was to take him back.

The young boy was determined to stay off that track. He wanted C.J., not his Father or Mother. C.J. wasn't just a new friend, he became in an instant, more like a brother. Back and forth the boy ran to and fro. But C.J. corralled him, I thought way to go little bro.

See, I forgot that all youth aren't here just to plunder and pillage. C.J. reminded me that some youth today, do help make a village.

LEAVE A MESSAGE

After the tone. Please leave a message.
That's all I ever hear; I didn't call to talk to a machine.

There is something I need you to hear.
Keeping it 100 you know what I am trying to say.
Leave a message at the beep is like the soup of the day.
Dare I say even cliché.

Answer the damn phone please.
That's what you'd want me to do.
If that works for me, it should easily work for you.

Communication is like a game I think it's called phone tag.
Some even liken it to a game known as capture the flag.
The funny thing is, I know you're there.
Looking at the machine with that dumb ass stare.

To get a hold of you
on that
I have become hell bent,
So, I hope you get this,
consider it message sent.

LET ME CALL YOU RIGHT BACK

If you hear those words, try to stay focused.
Gather your thoughts and get right back on track.
See, when you hear: Let me call you right back.
It usually means that they aren't quite through
with what they had to do.
Bottom line is, whatever she was doing is more important than you.

Damn that waiting by the telephone.
Picking up the receiver every ten seconds just to hear a dial tone.
You see, let me call you right back is part of life's little game that's played.
Still waiting on the call she'll claim she made.

Truth is, she did try to call you, but she got a busy signal
because you kept picking up the receiver.
Dogging the phone like a golden retriever.
Waiting for the phone to ring crouched, ready to pounce.
Taking every part of you not to pick up the phone
to call her, I mean every ounce.

Man, you know it' true. I'm the same way too.
Don't let I'll call you back mess with your head.
I won't tell brother, go on ahead.
Pick up the phone and just call her instead.

LET ME IN

Just where should I start?
Or let's say begin?
I don't know exactly just what happened.
I found myself with some girl.
My head in her lap.

Asking myself, where's the trap?
I knew it was a set up, you see.
So, I'm taking my time to make sure I tread lightly.

I asked myself.
Self, aren't you tired of slipping and falling?
You are 59 years old at this time in your life.
Brother you should be ballin.

All of my life I've been trying to win.
Changed up my game, trying to do it without sin.
I have a request, before my life comes to an end.
Asking for forgiveness, Father I promise.
I won't do it again.
Lord, can you open the door and please let me in.

LET ME INTRODUCE MYSELF

My name is Martin, A.K.A. Good Time Marty.
Somewhat true because I do like to party.
So, let me cut through the crap and let's get this thing started.
Trust me when I say, this comes from the heart.

I just want you to know I'm tired of the life that once was.
Also known as the freaking side show.
This facade you see, is not how I want you to view me.
Ole Good Time Marty ain't good for nothing but a good time.

Yeah, that's what an ex told me.
Not exactly the look I was going for her to have of me.
Known at times to drop a line.
That often times will blow your mind.

Have people saying things like "Boy you stupid, you crazy."
Hell, even got my Grandpa saying
"He ain't a millionaire because the boy lazy."

Once again, my name is Good Time Marty.
When I party best believe, I party hearty.
Know by reputation to get things started.
Start stuff sometimes, most definitely.

Known also to have your six in a fight.
Might be the mediator, making sure every thing's alright.
If you have a problem with what or who you see in me.

Remember one thing,
Good Time Marty A.K.A. Martin, I will always be.
Best believe That's cool with me.

LET ME TELL YOU

Let me tell you 'bout this girl named Tess.
Catch her on a bad day, might make you think:
Ooooooh, she a hot mess.

But here's the thing you might not see.
When she got it together, no finer thing could ever be.
Let me tell you about Tess.
Piss her off, boy it's gon be some stress.

Not on her, but damn sure on you.
So, let me tell you what you might want to do.
First thing, if you want to avoid a fight,
just admit she's always right.

That's because in her mind she is.
Let's just say, it is what it is.
Trust me, choose not to agree you gon get the biz.

Now don't get it twisted.
She got ya back this is true.
But if you fuck over her.
Guaranteed she'll fuck over you.

Another thing don't ever talk about her family or kids.
Then you will hear, see what you did?
Even when the vultures begin to circle,
the girl will start acting like Steve Erkle.
Look you dead in the eye talkin bout did I do that?

LIFE IS A RIVER

It runs long and deep. You need to know this when the waters look calm. Remember the rapids will come. When approaching, prepare to be jostled and tossed from side to side. If not trained properly, may just capsize.

Listen for the cry: "Man overboard" followed by: "Please help me, Lord" Life is a river. It can be a giver or a taker. A new birth identifier and a widow maker.

For that reason, it is crucial that you wear your life jacket. This vital piece of equipment when used correctly, enables you to hack it.

You will eventually come upon smooth waters. That is where you need to show and teach them how to navigate this river. I am speaking of your sons and daughters.

The rapids? They are sure to go through, hopefully paying attention to the lessons of me and you. Life is a river; they'll need to learn to maneuver.

Of lessons learned, if what's retained is but a sliver.

Joy, Peace, and Happiness this river called life is sure to deliver.

LIVE IN YOUR TRUTH

The king of liars, he is called by many.
When it comes to the truth told by him, you will not find any.
Because he tries to have you believe the real truth is a lie.
Listen to him and his truth and you will certainly die.

The truth that you know is the truth of life.
The king of lies plan is to attempt to distract.
He knows you know the real truth so it's you, he will attack.
His plan is to have God's truth you retract.

He does this by playing games with your mind.
He wants you to question the Father, where your truth you will find.
See, God your Father can not tell a lie.
There is no reason for him to or dare even try.

But with Satan, to lie is all he will do.
His sick world is perverted, filled with half-truths and illusion.
But in your truth, you serve a God, one that is not one of confusion.
His words and promises he gives to us freely
so that we may live in truth, knowledge, and wisdom.

So, in decisions you make there will be no division.
Your choices are sound, God's words are your proof.
So, do not be afraid to live in your truth.

MAGICAL

Oh yeah, that's what it started out to be.
Mom, Dad, and Sister close to me.
You see, in a perfect world all four together forever
it was supposed to be to me.

We were a family.
I had no idea that's not how it would turn out to be.
No longer four when Dad walked out the door.
Now cut down to three.
Problem was that wasn't the way it was supposed to be.

Magic was what I thought it would be.
Instead of magic, twists and turns made things tragic.
All of us attempting to be tactical.
To bring the family back together again.

Unfortunately, the tragedy once it started had no end.
To remain two households at the time just seemed to be practical.
Not at all what I envisioned.
Not part of my dream.
Didn't dream about practical.
This was supposed to be "MAGICAL".

ME, MYSELF, AND I YOUR WORST ENEMY?

Me, is who I would truly like to be.
Myself, well not so sure.
See, me can be somewhat selfish.
But when I'm myself, I become selfless.

I really can't see who me, and myself are truly supposed to be.
They were, at one time trying to be a team.
If you ask them individually, they'll say that's the dream,
a real dream-team.

They made an attempt.
They tried to unite.
When I stepped in, they began to fight.

The goal was to unite, not argue and fight,
together handle their biz.
Not this shit, it is what it is?

But I ignored me and myself.
United it seemed they would never be.
The truth is, if me, myself, and I don't get it together
from now 'til forever.

The chance of success, is probably never.
So, me, myself and I will give it one last try.

The goal is to unite and get this thing right.
Fact is united we stand and divided we fall.
Today me, myself, and I we are all for one and one for all.
Keep this up and again we shall stand tall.
Please don't be your own worst enemy.

MEASURE?

Love is filled with depth.

This fact you can't neglect.

You may have little,

sometimes too much.

My mind is puzzled, too much love?

Is there such?

How is it measured?

By sight or by touch?

Is it appeal or something you

feel? What is it's origin this thing called love? Can it be from depths below or is its descent from above? Whether it's sent from on high like a mountain steep or buried underground somewhere deep. Any love given or received should be considered a treasure. For true love is one thing that you just cannot measure.

MEMORY LANE

Memory lane. A street in my mind that I would like to revisit. The question is why memory lane? What's so special about it? what is it?

The truth is, I really don't know. Memory lane is a street my mind often travels. Problem is if I stop at the wrong address my whole world may unravel.

Memory Lane is a strange thing. You may not recall but for me the same old thing.

Having wandered up and down that particular street on Memory lane, a street filled with both joy and pain. A street where you never know, who you just might meet.

Why would you want to visit a place you've already been? A place filled with unpleasant memories and maybe some old friends? I told you, yes it had some pain but also a lot of joy.

At least that's my recollection as a little boy. Memories have your mind in a state of delusion craving that blast from the past, or was it just an illusion?

However, choosing to make that your first stop trying to get there fast. My advice, be careful, just make sure your first stop doesn't turn out to be your last.

So, if it's adventure you seek, may I suggest a future road. I believe it would be a great destination for you, you know, something fresh, something new.

Instead of Memory Lane, man get a clue; the corner of Present and Future Roads, that's the place for you.

There you will be sure to find your destiny.

Instead of traveling the same road searching for a memory.

MISS ME!

This if for all of you who attempt to dis me.

Whether it's woman, child, or man.

Don't you see? I'm doing the best that I can!

Miss me while you're sitting back chillin, relaxed wanna dis me?

You fake ass Mack.

Don't get me wrong, I have my faults.

Took a chance trying to crack some vaults.

You need to miss me, don't you see.

For trying to be me, might as well be a slave that'll never be free.

Dis me, how dare you speak.

Especially knowing your game is weak.

You need to step, for I make your dumb ass leak.

Put yo ass on a year long tweak.

Don't you ever again think once about trying to dis me.

I am the best thing since sliced bread.

Keep talkin shit fuck around get head spread.

Me you'll never be, so for the last time… Mutha Fucka Miss me.

MY MIND

My mind, what's wrong with it?
These days trying to find it.
Especially today.

It seems as someone has put it away,
like, hid it from me.

Realizing my mind seems not quite
what it used to be
what's left of it is.

Not knowing whether it's mine or his.
Constantly wondering,
I just can't figure it out.

Is it because it craves more?
It feels like it's less?
I've tried stimulation as well as simulation.

See, my mind now is questioning me.
Posing the question why
it's not what it used to be.

My mind appears to be somewhat frustrated,
I remember when it stayed elated.
Happy is what it craved to be.

I'll tell you one thing.
This mind can't belong to me.
On that, both me and my mind can certainly agree.

All I ask is what happened to mind?
Please can you help me find it.
I believe I've finally lost it.

MY MUSE

My muse is what she is to me.
The way our relationship started, not thought be.
Nevertheless, my Muse she turned out to be.

My Muse might not be the same to you
as she is to me.
Though my Muse,
thought that she would always be.

It turned out not that way for her.
See, my muse keeps my thoughts and focus pure.
One glance from her and everything is for sure.

My Muse, no longer I continue to hold out hope.
See, without my Muse can't seem to cope.
Yes, you heard right and yes, I said it.

Without my Muse.
Don't know where I'm headed.
I miss you LuLu.

NO LONGER

So, I am no longer a priority.

Don't know what made me think

I would ever be.

Was it the way she looked at me?

The way she walked, talked or had me look at life differently.

Part of her clan she tried to make me.

Blind to her eye, I became eventually.

She requested that I keep everything 100.

Until she realized what she wanted me to do.

Well, I had already done it.

This made me no longer her priority.

Question is, was I ever really meant to be?

Answer:

Apparently, not necessarily.

NO SIGNAL

I received no signal from you.
Informing me of what it was I was to do.
No return signal you claimed to receive from me.
Instructing you on what you were to be to me.

Without a signal there was no communication.
No signal sent or received leads to frustration.
What is the problem? Aren't we on the same station?

Could it be operator error?
Or something as simple as the weather.
We just went through a storm.
The cause unknown, the signal is lost.

Danger on the horizon.
No way to estimate the potential damage or cost.
Receiving no signal, we were both left to wonder.

How much trouble are we in?
Is our ship going under?
Who is the captain of this vessel in open waters we're sailing?

No land insight, just drifting; taking on water so fast
we need to start bailing.

Our vessel is sifting, lacking a signal our relationship's failing.
With no signal, I hope that you know Morse code.
May be the only thing left to save our humble abode.

You persist in thinking there's no signal, I've tried; can't you see?
So, try changing your channel and signal me.

#

One of the first words we learn.

NO.

No, don't touch that,

No, you can't have that.

No, you better not do that.

No, you can't say that, think that;

No, you can't be that.

No, don't believe that.

No, is you crazy?

No, you can't achieve that.

Never let the word no stop you.

The one thing I must confess, this much is true.

If you hear enough No's.

Put GOD first and you are headed for a life changing YES.

NOT HARD TO FIND

So, you say it's not hard to find.
Well, if that is true then I must be blind.
For a very long time I have searched for **Love, Peace, Joy and Happiness**. Not an easy task, I must confess. I was told by others with guidance and direction, seek and you will find. Just the overall concept of obtaining these gifts blows my mind.

But well, I guess I beak them down one by one. **God's love** is where all **Love** began. It started with his love affair with his ultimate creation, he chose to call man. **God** thought, to make him happy he would create man a mate. Someone with whom man could share **God's love** and appreciate. Not to subtract from, but to add to and equate. Everything was perfect for quite a while. Seeing man in **love** with woman caused God to smile.

To live happily ever after was the plan for thee. Until one bite of some fruit from a forbidden tree. Now you just keep that in mind. That's when **love** became hard to find. This brings us to **Peace**. This was a gift that was given by **God** as well. A state of being in which we were intended to dwell. A gift meant to be both yours and mine. In truth, it also became hard to find.

To be paired with **love and peace** it was supposed to be. Because of the betrayal of **God's love** by man and woman, the **Joy** once experienced by **God** would quickly flee. The **Joy** we were to receive from heaven above, at times is delayed. Because **God's love was betrayed**. Which brings us to the last part of this missing equation a thing called **Happiness**; often denied because of a serpent's persuasion.

This is what caused smiles and laughter to disappear. A gift once right in the palm of our hand, no longer near. You see, all these were created for us to enjoy, value, and hold dear. Operating through life without possessing these gifts. You can understand why it seems your life's somewhat a miss.
I can't speak for you, but I must insist I long for the feelings of **LOVE, PEACE, JOY** and **HAPPINESS**. I liken it to receiving from **God** himself a big warm hug and a gentle tender kiss.

See, **God's** blessings just seem to ease my mind. You'll realize that by holding his hand and believing in him. Keep this one thing in mind. These gifts from **God** given freely from above, **are not** hard to find especially <u>**HIS LOVE**</u>.

NOTHING BUT THE HITS

You don't always see them. But some days the hits just keep on coming. Left and right blows coming high and low. Hope you know how to counter punch? If not, the blows of life will eat you for lunch.

The punch may come from the I.R.S. the name alone can conjure up stress. While the loss of employment can make your life a bloody mess. Those two blows alone can cause some strife. Loss of confidence maybe your wife.

Blows hit so hard contemplating loss of life. I hate to bring this up almost forgot about infidelity. Life trying to set you up for a K.O. punch, called the felony. The pre-fight instruction, protect yourself at all times.

See, life don't fight fair. It plays by it's own rules. Bottom line: life just don't care. It will fight dirty, expect blows below the belt; hit you so hard dead ancestors felt.

Well, hope you're wise enough to see through the rhyme. In a fight with life, ain't no such thing as a bad time.

I guarantee the hits will continue to come. The fight plan is to have you throw in the towel and admit you're done. But don't give in, stand up and fight.

For the Father's in your corner, no need for fright. Instead, get on your knees and pray; for he promised that by your side he will always stay.

So, my brothers and sisters, don't give up the fight. Instead let GOD give you strength and all his might.

You might not win the round today. But with God in your corner, Life's knock out blows will be kept at bay.

NOW IS TEMPORARY

Not necessarily linked to your past or your future.
The first thing you need to understand is
tomorrow is not promised to any child, woman, or man.

Now at times it may seem
that your world is caving in on you,
and no matter how hard you try,
seems there is nothing you can do.

Trust me, I've been there, past due bills,
Unemployment, repossessed cars,
foreclosed mortgages, kids doing bad in school,
relationship problems…
You name it.

See, it may be this way today
overwhelming dare I say,
even a little bit scary.

Just remember this one important thing.
My friends, now is temporary.
Now give this some thought,
something said, done or imagined one second ago,
well, that is literally and figuratively in the past.

The same applies to one second from now.
Well, that is the future.
Hence now is temporary.
May I suggest, forget the past; it's something you can't change.

The future you may plan,
but more than likely done in vain.
Yesterday is history and tomorrow being a mystery.

Regarding this subject, I'm not trying to be contrary.
So, open your eyes and realize that now is so, so very temporary.

OBVIOUS

How did I miss that?

The answer was right in front of my face.

I can't believe it.

My head must have been in the wrong place.

I just don't quite understand.

Makes no sense to me,

must have had it buried in the sand.

This has my head swimming,

am I on the sea or dry land?

You can see it through a microscope yes, it's obvious.

I'm about to give up hope.

Thought to myself,

this just can't be me one look in the mirror;

it's me obviously.

Feeling the lack,

knowing there's so much more to me.

At least there was supposed to be.

I hope in me the confusion you can see.

If not, you must be blind obviously.

ON THE LINE

On the line, that's how I feel.
Come on my brothers.
Am I the one and only?
Don't leave me out here stranded and lonely.
Let me know if you ever felt like this.
At times don't you feel like a big mouth Bass?
Messed around and got hooked by the line she cast.
You can't get free from that hook.
Admit it, she didn't even use bait
all it took was one look.
Now recalling when you were swimming
through a sea of women.
Bait in hand guaranteed to catch at least one,
man, that was a given.
Once in an aquarium
now in a fishbowl your living.
Had you bragging
"Boy don't you know I'm winning".
You swore that was gospel and was a fact.
Until she took a closer look.
Measured you…
and threw your ass back.

ON TIME AND ON DEMAND

Yeah, I Know that is what you expect me to be.

Failing to realize that is just not me.

My question to you is: Why should I be?

Ordering me to be on time.

It is a good thing this is true.

But telling me, not asking:

Just who do you think you are talking to?

You see, the tone of your request comes off

like more of a command.

I must tell you frankly:

For that, this grown ass man will not stand.

So, address me correctly,

when on time

and on demand

is what you want me to be.

On time

and on demand

you better be.

Yo ass ain't the boss of me.

Oh, Ow, okay, okay Damn.

I'm sorry MaMa.

PIECES

My life appears to be in pieces.
Torn, shattered, and scattered,
like the pieces you might find
in an open puzzle box.

No idea of where to begin.
Looking at the picture
on the front of the box all the pieces came in.

No idea where to start
to put this puzzle called my life,
back together again.

Searching for the four corners
to help me begin.
Going methodically piece by piece
to see if it fits.

I think I found one wait, no that's not it.
Must regain my focus,
I lack concentration.

My way is just not working
often led to frustration.
Directions I follow
feel like miseducation.
Trying over and over
to piece it together.
Some pieces are missing,

You know what?
Whatever.
I search high and low for my life's missing pieces.
Sure, hope that I find them,
so, I will know what **TRUE PEACE IS.**

PITFALLS

Whether you want it or not.
Take a look around
and you'll see
a pitfall is what you've got.

Oh, I forgot to tell you.
Pitfalls hit us all.
They can bring trials and tribulations
to you and yours.

Can take you places

 you didn't want to go.

"Ask me why a pitfall?"

Honestly, I don't know.

Let's change the order of the word.

I wonder, what we'll find?

Falls pit, you see.

Falls in the pit.

Guarantee didn't see that one coming,

unplanned destiny.

So, wherever you land or happen to fall.

Always remember pitfalls hit us all.

RATHER HAVE A LOVE

I would rather have a love.
One like I've never known,
one that she and I could call our own.

You know, like an adventure
through the great unknown.
The destination one
where love is definitely shown.

Not just of the physical kind,
but also, the mental,
emotional and spiritual;
the type of love that's hard to find.

In my eyes,
everything the world has to offer
cannot compete
with that type of love.

For that type of love
must be sent from above.
You must understand.

The world says it has
whatever you can imagine,
whatever you can think of.

As for me,
this Man;
well,
I'd rather have a love.

REACH OUT

Do you remember:
"Reach out, reach out and touch someone?"
If not, well, that was the jingle for AT&T.
Made me think of how I love
when you reach out
and verbally touch me.

It's been a long time
since I've been touched by you
physically, mentally, or verbally.

Although my heart
still feels you spiritually.
From my body and mind
you may have strayed.

Yet your spirit
in mine has always stayed.
Though from each other
at this time, we're miles apart.

Let today
be the day
we make
a new start.

My love for you,
there is no doubt.
So, baby please,
won't you take the time
to reach out and touch me?

REALLY

Really, you say I'm using you.
Ask me if I am,
I believe you are using me too.

I mean really,
how am I supposed to live?
When all you do is take
and appears nothing you give.

You see,
you really only have one life to live;
really.

If you think about it
the most important thing
is not what you receive,
but to the table what you bring.

You can't just think
about you
and what it is
you want to do;
really.

Now hear this.
listen to what I have to say.
You should really
get down on your knees and pray.
For the revelation that things
won't always go your way.

That for now
is all I have
for you today.

REFILL

Seems the glass once full is now apparently empty.
I stepped away from my drink for what seemed like a minute.
Went to grab it trying to recall what was in it.
Believing it to be half full I reached for another swallow.
Not going to happen; see, my 16 once full glass turned out to be hollow.

Checked to see if there was a possible spill.
No, that didn't happen, no spill.
Went back to the bar and ordered a refill.
I ordered a different drink this time.
Wondering from this drink,
what I could possibly find.

This time to ease my mind.
See, my first drink was a mix of doom, gloom,
depression and a shot of despair.
Guzzled it down as if I didn't have a care.

Don't understand why I put that drink on my tab.
Couple more of those will definitely need a cab.
Looked at my bill: Man, that first drink was expensive.
No worries, I had a bad day with losses that proved extensive.

I tell you what the bartender said,
"Why don't you try this new drink? Called trust in me"
The taste was amazing I wondered what could it be.
This drink had a different flavor.
You know the type of drink designed to savor.

"Brah this drink's the shit, can you please do me a favor?
I need to know what's in it.
Man, it tastes like something sent from above.
I swear it taste like it was made with some love"

His answer was: "sure I'll even do that for free,
let me grab the cocktail book and will take a look".
"Well, it starts with a shot of new goals,
then we add some hope,
dreams topped off with just a pinch of possibilities"

"Wow that's sounds like the perfect drink for me"
"I must say I've never tried it"
One sip, my elation I couldn't hide it.

A lady at the bar asked: "Well, how does it taste?"...
"No need to answer it's written all over your face."

The glass was never empty. It never reached half full.
With this new drink, I couldn't wait to pay the bill.
If it ever gets close to empty guess what?
"Yo! Bartender can I please have a refill?"

If he happens to say:
"Sure, what will it be?"
"That's easy, I'll have another
Trust in Me."

REMARKABLE

I see it in you.
Can you see it in me?
The fact that we're remarkable?
Please, where do I begin?

If it's with you I could be.
Let me say I'm all in.
The way I see it is,
we both could win.

Remarkable,
don't you want to be?
Question is,
do you see a future?
For you and me?

Now, I'm not quite sure
if you see what I see.
But, you and me,
remarkable I bet we'd be.

RUNNING

I started out on a little jog.
My sunny day was hit by fog.
Looked left then right, then realized
not a landmark in sight.

See, the destination was
the house of the Lord.
He was the refuge I sought.

He was what I was looking for.
Running towards what I thought
was a landmark that seemed
to be calling out to me.

Turned out to be the enemy.
Leading down the wrong path
diverting me
from Thee.

Then, there was a light
that shined at my feet.
Shined by My Savior
my enemy he'd defeat.

The sun has returned
now I'm back
on the right path.

My mind, body, and spirit
my Father now has.
Running in circles all this time
I turned out to be.
After this day.
No more running for me.
Finally, in the arms of the Lord who
protects and keeps me.

SCARS

Scars, I believe we all have them.

Physical, mental even spiritual they may be.

Some scars so deep,

they're unrecognized by the naked eye.

The scars we bare, we hope avoid infection.

It takes a keen eye and a steady hand

to achieve external and internal perfection.

When treating the internal and the mental…

Well, let's just say you might need some direction.

Healing the heart, mind, and soul's scars

is quite different you see.

But with faith, hope and trust in God…

All your scars will be healed perfectly,

I guarantee.

SHARING IS CARING

I once knew this special girl.
One glance at her, well...
rocked my world.

Homies, lovers, friends we came to be.
Thought she was all about me,
turned out I was wrong.
I had to share you see.

I know you probably think
I 'm selfish.
Yeah, this may be.

See, I was not sharing
with just her family.
I was sharing with Ex's,
even the baby daddy's family tree.

Not even knowing
what happened to "We"
or, who I'd share with next.

One day I found myself paralyzed,
perplexed.
Standing in front of the mirror
numb just staring.
Then it hit me.
To her.
Sharing is caring.

SHEEPLE?

When did so many of God's people become the enemy's sheep?
They're called sheeple. Believing everything they hear.
Living every day in a state of fear.
You don't serve a God of fear!

No longer leaders. Just looking to follow.
It seems there's no common sense. Heads almost seem hollow.

Heeding the direction of every little Bo peep.
I thought they were God's people, but they acting just like sheep.
Following shepherds' wolves in sheep's clothing. Sent by the devil.

Not trying to be offending, I'm speaking directly
to the ones in the pulpit pretending.

You know who you are. Unfortunately, some sheeple know who they are too.

Looking to take what God created and just bring them down
to the devil's level. I consider them frienemies.

Leading God's children astray. Wrapped in a bow to deliver to the enemy.
A life of everlasting torture and torment eagerly awaits you.

Unless you follow the real shepherd whose word always rings true.
To follow him leads to a life everlasting. A simple life that contains
constant prayer and a little fasting.

But it seems that you choose to follow the one called Satan.
Then have the nerve to sit back crying and complaining.
Why not just fix your mind on becoming the Lord's disciple?
A fisherman of man, woman, and child.

Don't be the devil's follower. Be one of God's leaders.
Where you can stand tall and to the promise land lead God's people.
Rebuke the enemy's traps and snares. Remember you are one of God's soldiers you were born prepared.

Help defend the Father's throne. Never forget you are never alone.
You are a powerful member of his army. Stand up and be counted.

Be the true leader of Gods people he created you to be.
Resist the temptation and that urge, never forget Satan wants you
to just be sheeple.

Sheeple, I feel baaaaaaaaaad for you.
I am praying for your deliverance. Let the people of the LORD SAY SO!!!!!!
Remember whose image you are created in and don't you ever forget it.

In the name of Jesus. Take that bell from around your neck.
Put on your whole Armor and pick up your sword.

There is a war being waged against God's kingdom.
Calling all Christians.
"LET'S GET READY TO RUUUUUUMMMBBBLLE!"
Hallelujah! Amen, Amen and AMEN!!!

SILENCE YOU KEEP

The silence you keep can be deafening.
To some it speaks volumes.
Whereas, others wonder
what is that you are not saying.

You've learned
if open your mouth
and dare speak the truth.
You'll probably have problems
even when you have proof.

See, the silence you keep
may turn out to be your best friend.
It can save you from conversational issues
that lead to no end.

For me it is different.
Silent, I refuse to keep.
At times it creates
mountains to climb
some small and some steep.
For me it is not worth it
to not make a peep.
A vow to be silent
will not to keep.

SO NICE

Hey, you know, it was so nice to see you again. I've missed you. You once were my dearest friend. I'm not quite sure what happened or even where to begin.

I'm really glad that I'm not you. Ask me why, well it appears to me. Either you don't want to or refuse to see, just who everyone else expects you to be. Sorry to say, that includes even me.

Your dilemma is do you want to please you, or them? Just an observation of a longtime friend. You no longer have to people please, hell you don't even have to be nice.

Go by your gut and don't think twice. Now I've tried before to share with you this sound advice. You didn't listen then.

So, I hope you do now, and I pray things for you, work out right. Just remember you don't always have to be so nice.

SOMEONE NEW

"I met someone new"
is what I was told.
My question was:
Why is that you felt the need?

The vibe I got;
the need became apparent indeed.
A new stud it seems you need.

Prayed you wouldn't have the need
to replace me as your noble steed.
No longer your workhorse,
your thoroughbred.

Put out to pasture
when all was done and said.
I see the young quarter horse
turned your head.

It's great you found someone new
and I know there's nothing
more I can do.

No argument from me,
that would just be plain silly.
The truth of the matter is,
I found a brand-new Philly.

SPECULATION

Speculation causes thought.

A battle of the mind continuously fought.

Speculation makes you wonder what if?

Posing the question, is it a curse or a gift.

Through questions of speculation

you will be required to sift.

Trying to find the answers behind its doors,

speculation's puzzles may require more.

I hope that I am not alone,

and you too can relate.

Come one, come all!

Let's not be late.

Everyone, take a seat.

Let's speculate!

THAT'S ON YOU

Answer me this question.
Why is everyone trying to blame me
for what you've done?

Seriously, what was I supposed to do?
Complained about my behavior,
acted like I was some sort of savior.

Wanted me to be Mr. fix it, yes, it's true.
But you were reluctant
to let me use my skills to help you.

At the end of the day, let me say it this way:
You wouldn't let me do what I do.
Now you have problems,
you and your crew.

Said it's my fault but that's on you.
You created negative situations
driven by your own temptations.

Then have the nerve
to bring me your frustrations.
Listening to you know who,
knowing they didn't have a clue.
All I can say is:
That's on you.

THE DIFFERENCE

The difference is: If you have one before the other, what's next?

See If you start with love, the next question will probably be:

When will he or she have sex with me?

Now, let's start with sex the question.

That will probably be next.

Does he or she love me?

What if there's neither one for me?

You see either or, or both; great it would be.

Truth is, at this time love or sex for me,

would lead to problems eventually.

You see, sex is the equivalent of a four letter feel good.

Where love is a four letter, I wonder if I should.

See, for me there is a difference between love and sex.

However, both lead to the same question, which is:

What's next?

They seem to lead to one thing,

it always seems to be.

One: is a different you;

and two: is a different me.

EYES OF A CHILD

Through the eyes of a child
I wish I could see.
Just a better view
of what life could possibly be.

The eyes of a child are filled
with amazement and wonder.
Wondering, what it is they see?
and all the possibilities.

Through the eyes of a child
they see and think
that the world is mild.

There are few chores,
no job, no stress.
Treating everyday
like it's their birthday.

I don't jest.
Sometimes even allowed
to make a mess.
The one thing that I must confess,
through the eyes of a child
I realize I'm blessed.
For I am God's child.

THE LIFE OF A BLACK MAN

The life of a Black man seems the hardest. A life where his dreams often seem the farthest. His life involves struggle, also some pain. Though many may struggle a few find fame. Fame that most times is fleeting, disappearing so fast it looks as if he's retreating.

Ain't it a shame, we don't even remember his name. A life that's so difficult, he daily asked why? I can't gain any ground, so why even try? See, the life of some Black men have them questioning their women. Asking "do you know what it is like to me?

Slavery was over centuries ago; didn't they say I was free?" Still singing old Negro spirituals wondering will success and prosperity ever find me? Things so bad the Police have me afraid to drive my car. Pulling me over on the regular, like I just left the bar. Mutha Fucka please. Talkin shit bout "Where you hide the trees?"

"Sir I'm just getting off work, wait one minute while I reach slowly for my I.D." A Police involved shooting victim, Lord please don't let me be. "Yes officer, I have registration and Insurance" "I just told you sir I work for a living"

"Please step out of the car" A request often heard. "Place your hands on the hood, spread your legs, take a seat on the curb" See, the Police around here got a Black Man living in constant fear. Things getting so bad make you want to shed a tear.

Killing Brothers and Sisters year after year. Hunting them down like it is open season. Courts let them off like they didn't need a reason. The life of the Black man some might say. "I wouldn't want to live that life even on a good day".

You may question just why is that? Well, in his life just to survive is a struggle. Waking every day of his life just trying to avoid the PoPo and trouble. The life of a Black Man tends to be filled with heartache and pain.

A life where no one but five-o wants to know your name. Yeah, I know, it's a got damn shame. Like I said before sometimes this life makes you want to shed a tear.

Dreams of his children's future he fights to hold dear. He doesn't want his seed to have to endure this shit. You damn right, not one bit. For his family he puts in hardwork and dedication. With hopes of one day helping to change this nation.

So, don't get frustrated; don't you dare shed one tear.

You see, because when the Black Man dreams,

he dreams **His dream** that much near.

THE POWER WITHIN

At times it seems
we can't seem to find it.
Sit, be still, be quiet and reminded.
Trust in the Lord
you'll find power restored.

He is the key for the power is he.
He's what it takes
to help your power flourish.
Meditate and pray the power of his spirit
your soul he will nourish.

Guaranteed to happen,
now let us begin.
Reach out to God
for your power within.

THE TRUTH ABOUT LYING

Truth is, lying is something that I often felt was necessary to do. Believing it would be better to lie, I believe that experience we all have been through.

I know I have lied and if you tell the truth, you probably have too. Funny thing is, to tell the truth or a lie is totally up to you.

I seemed to have no control over lying. Seemed telling the truth I would always in up in trouble. Found lying was worse because when caught in a lie my trouble was double.

Telling the truth couldn't do so with a lie I replaced it. Lying instead of being truthful often chose to replace it. To this day still don't understand why I lied.

Could be told face to face, by phone or a letter. Couldn't tell the truth if I tried, seemed the more that I lied, at it, I appeared to get better.

Why not just tell the truth? you say: "Wouldn't that be easier"? Not if she knew what I was up, to the truth wouldn't please her. Continued to believe it would appease her.

Then one day told a lie just too good to be true. Problem this time, was required to show proof. Once again caught in a lie, this one the Granddaddy of them all.

Like humpty dumpty great was my fall. A fall from the heights One of the Empire States roof. The lessons been learned, so I'll just stick to the truth.

THIS LIFE

This life, my life not what I expected it to be.
In speaking with you, now I can plainly see.
This life was not planned by neither you nor me.
Turns out this life is truly what you make it.

Can put you through so many things.
Your best bet is to learn how to take it.
One thing for sure about this life is you just can't fake it.

Also work really hard and please don't forsake it.
It is in your best interest to always try to make it.
Forget the stress, remember you're blessed.

This life may turn out to be lucky for you and me.
With the help of the Lord, you will finally see
that this life turned out
just like it was supposed to be.

TIME MARCHES ON

Your left, your left, your left, right left.

That's the cadence you were told to march to.

You learned early in life that time waits for no one.

Why you stand still it keeps marching on.

Time will continue to march

until your very last breathe.

Marching on until the day of your death.

Don't misunderstand and please don't forget.

Time marches on and on that you can bet.

Your left, your left, your left right left.

Time marches on

until you have nothing left.

March on.

TIME TO MOVE ON

Time to move was said to me.

Not by one, not two, not three, not even four.

Shamed to say it was probably more.

So often said could no longer ignore.

Once again told it's time to move on.

These four words, spoken by women in a relationship with me.

I tried my best lines, thinking all would be fine.

They refused to hear me these women of mine.

Using lines, they had never heard, told by one that I was absurd.

Another had said she talked with her mother.

Who persuaded my woman to go find another.

One even told "You think you're so clever"

Laughed in my face and just said "Whatever".

The last friend of mine

told me my mojo was gone.

Thought to myself,

Man, it's time to move on.

TIRED

I have always lived my life my Father to please.
I've prayed and cried tears, worn faith on my sleeve.
A mountain of belief I have in my soul.
My trust in him so strong it has broken the mold.

You see, when it comes to faith in my Father,
there are is rival.
Counting daily on him for my existence and survival.
Anxiously waiting for life to get better.
"Stay prayed up."
Followed instructions perfectly, to the letter.

They say "Without constant prayer
just think where you'd be."
No progress in sight is all that I see.
Prayer that once filled me with joy has now become labor.
I feel with my Father, I no longer have favor.

As I sit here praying, I must confess,
enduring the day to day grind
dreading having to face another of life's tests.

Had feelings of being abandoned by he,
left all alone, long suffering you see.
Trick of the devil I guess you might say.

In my mind it's all real,
not just another challenge of the day.

See, it seems this battle has lingered for years.
Filling my life with sorrow and fears.
Where is the peace, the love and the joy?
Good things happening for me, seem only a ploy.

The war waged against me seems personal.
Faith waning, strength draining.
Actions resemble a person hormonal.

For some time, the same dreams, and goals
I've had for my life.
Seems all I receive is toil and strife.

I give up, no more prayer for me, it does nothing.
Intercessors tell me
"Be quiet, you know you're just bluffing."

I guess the time to believe for me, has expired.
Sorry to say I'm refusing to pray
can't do it no more.
I'm tired.

TOO OLD TO LIVE FOREVER

Once there was a young man who dreamed like many do.
But his dream was to live forever.
His life was one of sunshine and lots of stormy weather.
In fact, he spent most of his life trying to get it together.

Believing that life could not get any worse,
it just had to get better.
He did not realize life's burdens could
be tougher than leather.

See, as a child life's burdens were as light as a feather.
Things like the love of his life,
needless to say, no longer together.
One he was sure would last forever.

Homes, cars, and great opportunities have come and gone.
At one time it is true, he had it all.
Then he set his dream up to take a terrible fall.
Tallying the wins in his life as well as the losses.
Lack of wisdom, too much folly turned out, would cost him. Sunshiny days will he see again? Not ever.
His reality is he is too old to live forever.

TRIED TESTED AND TRUE.

That's what I believe I am. How about you? Do you see yourself as tried, tested and true? One who is always inspired, searching for that fire.

The one that will bring out the best in me. Tried, tested and true, man if you only knew. Alcohol and drug addiction rendered me helpless with a true affliction.

Back in the day it was a thing called crack that derailed me. Completely throwing life off track. Then there were the women. Even though married I was still swimming in.

My life went through so many changes, I didn't know where the insanity began or if it would ever end. You know there is a problem when adultery and addiction become your best friends.

One thing I knew was this way of life could no longer continue. There where so many more delectable treats to enjoy on my life's menu.

What do you plan to do? I Shook my head, hands thrown up in the air answering, "I have no idea". Don't even have a clue? Without hesitation sensed my own frustration.

This what I was told by you. "You've tried everything else"."You've even tried by yourself". "Knowing that you can't depend on you". "The answer is clear. You need to get near to the one known to be tried, tested and true".

This was new to me. I asked "Who could that be? For this person is not known to me". "Oh yes you know him, he was once your closest friend until through your sin, you abandoned him.

I don't recall a friend at all, I would ever consider my closest. Think long and hard. It was the life of a brother called Moses in which he was in charge.

"This can't be true. Not after all that I've been through. There's just no way he would help me. His word is his proof. He's known for his truth.

He promised to never leave nor forsake thee. So, hear what I say. "Hit your knees now and pray".

You know what to do and if you want what's best for you. Put your pride aside and call on the one who is tried tested and true.

Christ Jesus, where are You? I can't do it no more. Lord, please help me through. I believe in you and that you are truly the one who is Tried, Tested and True.

Thank you Jesus for Loving me. Even when I didn't love myself.

TRUTH IS IT BEAUTIFUL?

All truth is beautiful, some might say.
The truth is, truth has a way of bringing the ugliness out of us all.
To tell the truth I believed was my duty.
Started to tell it but it quickly lost its beauty.

Please tell the truth always not sometimes you see.
At age 59 I feel the truth has been revealed to me.
One thing for sure is that all truth has beauty.

This can be hard to accept.
One thing about truth:
You never know what to expect.

See, at my age I finally had the opportunity
to see truth's beauty in action.
Let's just say I'm surprised.
Can't you tell by my reaction?

Reason is all these years I've found the truth
where there was nothing but lies.
Continue to dig deep
you'll find the truth and decipher the lies.
To tell the truth, is your duty.
So, steer clear of the lies
and recognize truth's real beauty.

TWO VS. ONE

The good Lord gave us two ears and one mouth. The simple math is so we can listen twice as much as we talk, no doubt.

Even though there is only one of them. Some have the ability to talk out of both sides of it.

Mouth running so much, just seems it can't quit. While the ears used to hear can't tune in to hear shit.

Not listening to anything you're talking about. No interest at all it seems to appear. Even with two good ears they ass still can't hear.

It's almost as if they were born deaf. When speaking almost like the palate's cleft.

Listening's skills no question, inept. With all their words, you know will be lies. Ask them to say: "Ahhh, just to see what's inside"

Just as I thought you got a forked tongue. With a mouth that won't stop talking until the day is done.

See, that forked tongue maybe good for French kissing. You'd be better off to be quiet, use those two ears and listen.

More than likely realize all you've been missing.

UNRIVALED

Unrivaled, is how I would describe a Mother's love.

The love she shares is hers and hers only.

If you're an outsider you're guaranteed to be lonely.

She is always at service to the ones she bore.

Devotion unrivaled need I say more?

You may try to fit in but that is difficult to do.

Disturb her cubs and you will see a true animal.

Get on her wrong side you'll believe she's a cannibal.

Take it from me and believe that it's true.

Don't be around when she starts to spew.

If you pose a threat, I feel sorry for you.

For you she will devour you.

The goal is for her to eat you alive.

For no one on earth can keep her cubs from her side.

See, they are the ones she is teaching to thrive.

Her young ones are truly her joy and her pride.

So, heed my advice for it may determine your survival.

Stay away from her cubs and realize Mama Bear is unrivaled.

VALENTINE/ ANNIVERSARY

I chose to write about Valentine's day.
A day for love for some, so they say.
I see this day in my very own way.
In a few words let me simply say.
Yes, for you it's Valentine's day.
For me it's February 14th. you don't say.

See, I almost forgot to you it's very special.
Today it's also special to me, about a love not necessarily.
You may ask: Why not?
Huh, well let me see.
Since you insist on questioning me.
All you're doing is pushing me further.

Okay well since you must know, on this day was a murder.
The victim was my sister, man I sure do miss her.
You see, she was one of two children
with a smile so bright and wide you just couldn't resist her.

The crime not solved to this day even they know the player.
Is said his name was Terrell found not guilty of being her slayer.

So, go ahead enjoy your flowers and your candy.
February 14th another day is all it is to me
and my broken family.

WALK AWAY

Sometimes you just might need to walk away.
Life every now and then throws things at you
that may resemble a pop quiz.
I'm just saying you never know
what each day will bring.

It could just be the same old thing.
Every now and then I don't really know.
Life can hit you with a devastating blow.
Could affect your relationship,
employment even your finances.

More than likely something bad.
Because life doesn't always bless you
with second chances.
The type that can change
life's circumstances.

Often times in life you
might have to pull yourself
up from the canvas.
It could be every day.

Have you wondered:
Should I go or should I stay?
If it were me, I humbly say,
continuously pray
and as long as there is a God
don't you ever quit
or walk away.

WALK WITH ME

That's what I heard him say.
Take my hand let me show you the way.
The path of peace, joy, and happiness
If may humbly say.

"Yeah right" is what I, sarcastically said.
Then a thought with a spark entered my head.
"Who are you to say that
you are the one
to show me the way"?

His response was given with boldness and confidence.
To that question my child,
I will take no offense.
I am the Alpha and the Omega;
and when it comes to the enemy,
I am your only defense.

I said: "Wait, hold up, what did you just say?"
"Now you heard what I said, and don't you forget it"
"If you don't take my hand, you'll surely regret it"

"You're on the wrong path my son, can't you see?
Now don't fuss,
Just trust"
"Take my hand, walk with me.
If done my son on this believe me.
Peaceful, Joyful and Happy you will be.
Not just for now but for eternity"

WHAT I'D LIKE TO DO

I wish I really knew.

Quiet has kept on life I've slept just trying to be true.

One thing that I'd like to do is stop living like a slob.

Oh, and let us remember divorce my useless mob.

I have this dream, one day will bring me some enjoyment

and one more thing, a song to sing when I secure employment. See, the last one I had, my own hands caused it to be taken.

I must admit that job I quit; a blessing forsaken.

Now I have some goals to set, especially ones yet to be met.

Due to a lifestyle that up, it would not let.

So, I will my mind's hope of peace to find.

Just let go, set it free.

Between me and you the plan is to thine own self be true.

I think that's what I'd like to do.

WHAT IS IT YOU WANT?

I'm asking because I'm just trying to figure it out. If your eyes and ears were open. You would hear and see, that what it is you want, truly matters to me. Is it love, joy peace or happiness?

Your desires of me have me somewhat perplexed. You say you want this, then you want that. Constantly changing your mind has me trying to guess what's next.

It seems you don't know what you want from me. I hope the day will come you clearly know and see. What you want is this up and down relationship to be.

WHAT WILL YOU GAIN WHEN YOU LOSE?

A newfound respect for the pain

experienced for the gain.

While on a lifelong, quest to maintain.

The goal.

To obtain all you have ever dreamed of.

While thoughts of loss, place a strain on your brain. From all potential excuses you have learned to abstain.

See, with life you will often lose more than you gain. Things like your health, your wealth;

too many losses may even lose yourself.

All this being said,

just wondering if pain you will choose.

At the end of the day.

What will you gain when you lose?

WHAT'S THE TRUTH?

The truth is today I hate you and you hate me.
Never imagined this is how our love would be.
Once, long ago, our love seemed to sizzle.
Now it's grown cold, the fire, it fizzled.

Truth is I never would say,
you know what?
screw you.
The reply being,
oh, is that so?
well screw you too.

Our love lacks sacrifice and humility.
Without these components.
Love has no ability.
Truth, is you don't respect me
and I refuse to respect you.
Tired of these mind games.

So, what are we going to do?
You no longer love me,
and I can't stand you.
Yell all you want,
you can scream to the roof.
Love is no more
and that is the truth.

WHEN LOVE STORMS OUT

After love storms out of the door.
Will you still hold on to what is no more?
Will you search to find somebody new?
When love storms out;
tell me just what will you do?

Now that love is gone,
can you see yourself making a new start?
Knowing that when it left,
love took a big piece of your heart.

Can you be true to someone new?
who has no clue?
Of just what love storming out
has done to you?

A love that your mind and heart strongly desire to be a part.
Of the one you shared your all in all.
That love that made you feel ten feet tall.
A love which never wavered through it all.

All the good times and the bad.
The love that made you happy when you were sad.
This love that you had never experienced before.
But everything changed
when love stormed out the door.

Will you just sit and wonder why love left you?
Why your love was denied?
Was it recognized that you really tried?
You are not even sure if you can love anymore.

Another victim turned out to be.
I feel sorry for you.
But I'm glad it's not me.

A victim of loss love, one that was pure.
Vow you did to love again.
This time make sure,
the next love is your closest friend.
All so that you can ensure.
That never again,
will love storm out the door.

WHERE DO I FIT IN?

I just thought I'd ask.
This is because I committed one of the ultimate sins.
One of our heavenly Father's top ten.
If you're wondering which one of the ten it just might be.
Simply put: Adultery.
From an unhappy marriage I long to be free.
Found someone that I thought would be she and me.
From a twenty-year sentence of a marriage the Judge released me.
Into the arms of another I chose to be.
Free at last, I thought I was don't you know.
I thought we'd last forever.
Little did I know.
A love unconditional I dreamed it would be.
I came to realize she valued a lot more than me.
The fact she was a single mom.
At the time made no difference to me.
Until I learned children more important than me.
All the while believing I had been released from my marriage.
One that I labeled the penitentiary and justice miscarriage.
Don't know where to begin on just how naive I had been.
Now asking why?
Why did you sin?
Second question asking my new Warden.
Just where do I fit in.

WHERE'D HE GO?

I once knew this brother.
I just can't seem to recall his name.
It's been said he never changed it.
So, it has to be the same.

They say it's the same as it used to be.
My question was where did he go?
I for one for sure don't know.
You have to know just where he'd be.

They said, "You don't know?"
That just can't be true.
I replied: Why's that?
Because he is you.

One last thing I just like to know.
Had to ask myself, bro.
Where did you go?

WITCH

That's what you turned out to be.
You deserve kudos, you surely bewitched me.
Call it my mistake, can even say my bad.
An angel heaven sent, is what I thought I had.

You caught me in a snare it turns out, you see.
A trap cast by your feminine wilds,
a spell released upon me.

Heartless, conniving, spiteful just plain evil.
Instead, you turned out to be.
Arguing over silly things anything you'd see.

Tricks so amazing and tremendous,
star crossed you had me.
Mystical words you spoke
seemed to come from afar.
Shepherd for the devil
and the spawn of Satan you are.

Your lies so believable,
did you pass the bar?
Painful, hurtful,
despicable words your anthem.

Good witch Glenda,
you're not trying to be.
Wicked witch of the west
I must confess
that's who you are to me.

WORTH TALKING ABOUT?

It has been said if you're new
you just may not know.
I'm worth talking about.
Even though, you may not think so.

There is one fact
that is definitely for sure.
There is much about me
you don't even know.

If I can spare the time,
I may just share with you.
What has been said about me
that I know is a lie
and what is very true.

Now if you take your time
you may just figure out.
If they're still talking about me.
Then I must be worth talking about.

YEAH

Yeah is a word you probably hear often.
Could be used to egg you on,
or in a disagreement
to try and soften the situation
of what is about to happen next.
So, let's take a look at this familiar text.

Yeah that's it,
I've had enough.
I'm tired of hearing
the same old stuff.

Yeah that's messed up
what they did to you.
Glad I wasn't with you,
that could have been me too.

Yeah boy it's going down,
they about to fight.

Yeah well, he doesn't want none,
at least not tonight.

Yeah that's what I thought,
you may just hear.
Followed by Yeah, that fool is lit
he doesn't need another beer.
Yeah, well I'm hungry bro.
What about you?

Yeah, I could grub,
let's see if we can find
something to hug on too.

Yeah is a word used way too much,
I must confess.
I think it's about time we stopped saying **Yeah**
and just start saying **YES!!!!!**

YOU KNOW THAT YOU WRONG

Yeah that's right I said it.
Things were all cool and going just right.
Watched you come in and started a fight.
I used to do the same thing,
an excuse for me to leave
and stay out all night.

Enter the house just like the Tasmanian devil,
start with something small
 and took it to a different level.
I mean a whole different level.
Where no one else wanted to be.

I recognize it because
You just used the same trick
to start a fight with me.
So, I will keep this thing short.
I'm not trying to be long.
That crap that you're doing,
you know that you wrong.

YOU MADE ME FEEL

You made me feel as if our love was real.
My mind and heart I allowed you to steal.
You came and left like a thief in the night.
I gave you the power to make me believe
everything was alright.

You made me feel like I was your King.
Mesmerized my thoughts of you being my Queen.
While at the same time,
you allowed others to come between.

You let them speak
making them an audience to be heard.
You told me, we'd always be,
you gave me your word.
I gave you my word
I admit I loved you.

No matter what happens
I'd always be true.
Keeping your word that you gave me,
you failed to do.

You had me believing that dreams can come true.
The words and the actions of you and your crew.
Made me feel like a fool.

Looking back,
I should've done the same thing to you.

YOU'RE NOTHING TO ME. UNTIL YOU ARE EVERYTHING.

Ultimately, I had no idea
what your so-called love for me would bring.
Would it bring joy and laughter?
Or hurt and pain?
Believe me when I say:
You are nothing to me,
until you are everything.

I don't need just some part of you.
Pieces of you just won't do.
Dare I say I must have all of you.

My life is not complete,
all your love I can't live without.
In my heart and my mind there is no doubt.

I'd hoped you'd be my everything.
Was prepared to secure that with a ring.
Turned out, you were to be just a fling.
Nothing resembling my everything.
Fooled once again by love
I turned out to be.

I did it as the last form which symbolizes that I finally got the book written!

www.ingramcontent.com/pod-product-compliance
Lightning Source LLC
LaVergne TN
LVHW020442070526
838199LV00063B/4817